1940 U.S.

YEARBOOK

ISBN: 9781090837417

This book gives a fascinating and informative insight into life in the United States in 1940. It includes everything from the most popular music of the year to the cost of a buying a new house. Additionally there are chapters covering people in high office, the best-selling films of the year and all the main news and events. Want to know who won the World Series or which U.S. personalities were born in 1940? All this and much more awaits you within.

FIRST EDITION

1940

January

S	M	T	W	T	F	S
	1	2	3	4	5	6
7	8	9	10	11	12	13
14	15	16	17	18	19	20
21	22	23	24	25	26	27
28	29	30	31			

◐:1 ●:9 ◑:17 ○:24 ◐:31

February

S	M	T	W	T	F	S
				1	2	3
4	5	6	7	8	9	10
11	12	13	14	15	16	17
18	19	20	21	22	23	24
25	26	27	28	29		

●:8 ◐:16 ○:23 ◐:29

March

S	M	T	W	T	F	S
					1	2
3	4	5	6	7	8	9
10	11	12	13	14	15	16
17	18	19	20	21	22	23
24	25	26	27	28	29	30
31						

●:8 ◐:16 ○:23 ◐:30

April

S	M	T	W	T	F	S
	1	2	3	4	5	6
7	8	9	10	11	12	13
14	15	16	17	18	19	20
21	22	23	24	25	26	27
28	29	30				

●:7 ◐:15 ○:21 ◐:29

May

S	M	T	W	T	F	S
			1	2	3	4
5	6	7	8	9	10	11
12	13	14	15	16	17	18
19	20	21	22	23	24	25
26	27	28	29	30	31	

●:7 ◐:14 ○:21 ◐:28

June

S	M	T	W	T	F	S
						1
2	3	4	5	6	7	8
9	10	11	12	13	14	15
16	17	18	19	20	21	22
23	24	25	26	27	28	29
30						

●:5 ◐:12 ○:19 ◐:27

July

S	M	T	W	T	F	S
	1	2	3	4	5	6
7	8	9	10	11	12	13
14	15	16	17	18	19	20
21	22	23	24	25	26	27
28	29	30	31			

●:5 ◐:12 ○:19 ◐:27

August

S	M	T	W	T	F	S
				1	2	3
4	5	6	7	8	9	10
11	12	13	14	15	16	17
18	19	20	21	22	23	24
25	26	27	28	29	30	31

●:3 ◐:10 ○:17 ◐:25

September

S	M	T	W	T	F	S
1	2	3	4	5	6	7
8	9	10	11	12	13	14
15	16	17	18	19	20	21
22	23	24	25	26	27	28
29	30					

●:2 ◐:8 ○:16 ◐:24

October

S	M	T	W	T	F	S
		1	2	3	4	5
6	7	8	9	10	11	12
13	14	15	16	17	18	19
20	21	22	23	24	25	26
27	28	29	30	31		

●:1 ◐:8 ○:16 ◐:24 ●:30

November

S	M	T	W	T	F	S
					1	2
3	4	5	6	7	8	9
10	11	12	13	14	15	16
17	18	19	20	21	22	23
24	25	26	27	28	29	30

◐:6 ○:14 ◐:22 ●:29

December

S	M	T	W	T	F	S
1	2	3	4	5	6	7
8	9	10	11	12	13	14
15	16	17	18	19	20	21
22	23	24	25	26	27	28
29	30	31				

◐:6 ○:14 ◐:21 ●:28

PEOPLE IN HIGH OFFICE

Franklin D. Roosevelt
President - Democratic Party
March 4, 1933 - April 12, 1945

Born January 30, 1882 and commonly known by his initials FDR, he served as the 32nd President of the United States until his death on April 12, 1945.

76th United States Congress

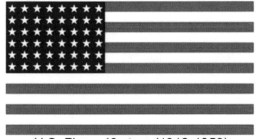

U.S. Flag - 48 stars (1912-1959)

Vice President - John Nance Garner	
Chief Justice - Charles Evans Hughes	
Speaker of the House	William B. Bankhead
	Sam Rayburn
Senate Majority Leader - Alben W. Barkley	

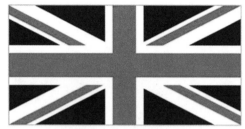

United Kingdom

King George VI
Dec 11, 1936 - Feb 6, 1952

Prime Minister
Neville Chamberlain
Conservative Party
May 28, 1937 - May 10, 1940

Prime Minister
Winston Churchill
Conservative Party
May 10, 1940 - Jul 26, 1945

Australia

Canada

Ireland

Prime Minister
Robert Menzies
United Australia
Apr 26, 1939 - Aug 28, 1941

Prime Minister
Mackenzie King
Liberal Party
Oct 23, 1935 - Nov 15, 1948

Taoiseach of Ireland
Éamon de Valera
Fianna Fáil
Dec 29, 1937 - Feb 18, 1948

Argentina

President
Roberto María Ortiz (1938-1942)

Brazil

President
Getúlio Vargas (1930-1945)

China

Premier
Chiang Kai-shek (1939-1945)

Cuba

President
Federico Laredo Brú (1936-1940)
Fulgencio Batista (1940-1944)

Egypt

Prime Minister
Aly Maher Pasha (1939-1940)
Hassan Sabry Pasha (1940)
Hussein Sirri Pasha (1940-1942)

France

President
Albert François Lebrun (1932-1940)
Vacant (1940-1944)

Germany

Chancellor
Adolf Hitler (1933-1945)

India

Viceroy of India
Victor Alexander John Hope (1936-1943)

Italy

Prime Minister
Benito Mussolini (1922-1943)

Japan

Prime Minister
Nobuyuki Abe (1939-1940)
Mitsumasa Yonai (1940)
Fumimaro Konoe (1940-1941)

Mexico

President
Lázaro Cárdenas (1934-1940)
Manuel Ávila Camacho (1940-1946)

New Zealand

Prime Minister
Michael Joseph Savage (1935-1940)
Peter Fraser (1940-1949)

Russia

Communist Party Leader
Joseph Stalin (1922-1952)

South Africa

Prime Minister
Jan Smuts (1939-1948)

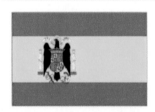

Spain

Prime Minister
Francisco Franco (1938-1973)

Turkey

Prime Minister
Refik Saydam (1939-1942)

U.S. NEWS & EVENTS

JAN

January 5 - Hollywood actors William Powell and Diana Lewis are married on a ranch near Las Vegas, Nevada. The marriage, just three weeks after they met, was a surprise to most people as few even knew they were a couple. *Fun facts: Lewis was Powell's third wife and they remained married until his death aged 91, in 1984.*

12	NBC initiates its first network television programming. A play called 'Meet the Wife' is broadcast to a station in Schenectady, New York.
14	FBI agents arrest 17 members of the Christian Front for planning a vast plot to overthrow the U.S. government and establish a fascist dictatorship. *Follow up: In reality their cache of weapons included an old saber and an 1873 Springfield rifle. One government official admitted off the record that the Front was really being prosecuted for un-Americanism. The jurors proved sympathetic to the defendants and returned no verdict - the government dropped its charges in 1941.*
14	The reigning NFL champions, the Green Bay Packers, beat an all-star team 16-7 in the National Football League's second All-Star Game at Gilmore Stadium in Los Angeles in front of 18,000 fans. The players on the all-star squad were selected by a national poll of fans.
22	The U.S. Treasury publishes a list of Americans who made salaries of more than $75,000 in 1938. The list revealed that Claudette Colbert was the highest-paid star in Hollywood that year with a salary of $301,944, followed by Warner Baxter who made $279,807.
26	Actor Norman Kerry joins the French Foreign Legion. He returns to the U.S. only after France capitulates to Nazi Germany.
28	A new musical quiz show called Beat the Band premieres on NBC Radio - The audience sent in riddles to the house band to which the answer was always the title of a song. Listeners earned $10 if their question was used on the show and an additional $10 if their question stumped the band.

4	The United States and Saudi Arabia establish full diplomatic relations for the first time when Bert Fish presents his credentials as American Envoy Extraordinary and Minister Plenipotentiary.
7	RKO Radio Pictures premieres Walt Disney's second full-length animated film, Pinocchio, at the Center Theater in New York City (the first full length animated Disney movie was Snow White And The Seven Dwarfs in 1937).

February 9 - Joe Louis defeats Arturo Godoy by split decision at Madison Square Garden in New York City to retain his Ring and world heavyweight boxing titles. He would defend these titles a further 3 times in 1940 against Johnny Paychek, Arturo Godoy (rematch), and Al McCoy. *Interesting facts: In all, Louis made 25 defenses of his heavyweight title from 1937 to 1948, and was a world champion for 11 years and 10 months. His most remarkable record is that he knocked out 23 opponents in 27 title fights, including five world champions. Photo 1: Godoy and Louis on CBS Radio's We, the People human interest program. Photo 2: Louis and Godoy in their rematch on June 20 - Louis won by a technical knockout in the eighth round.*

20	Tom and Jerry make their debut in the short film Puss Gets the Boot (under their original names of Jasper and Jinx). The cartoon was directed by William Hanna, Joseph Barbera and Rudolf Ising, and produced by Rudolf Ising and Fred Quimby.
27	Martin Kamen and Sam Ruben discover the radioactive isotope carbon-14 at the University of California Radiation Laboratory, Berkeley. *Interesting fact: Its presence in organic materials is the basis of the radiocarbon dating method pioneered by Willard Libby and colleagues (1949) to date archaeological, geological and hydrogeological samples.*
29	The 12th Academy Awards, celebrating the best in film from 1939, are held in Los Angeles and are hosted by Bob Hope (his first of nineteen ceremonies). Gone With The Wind won eight awards including Best Picture. Robert Donat and Vivien Leigh won the best actor and actress awards, and Hattie McDaniel became the first African-American to win an Oscar when she was named Best Supporting Actress. *Fun facts: The Los Angeles Times published the names of the winners in its 8:45pm edition so most of the attendees already knew the results ahead of time. The Academy responded by starting a tradition the following year in which the winners were not revealed until the ceremony itself when sealed envelopes were opened.*

2	The cartoon character Elmer Fudd (voiced by Arthur Q. Bryan) makes his debut in the Merrie Melodies animated short Elmer's Candid Camera.
6	Detective Comics No.38 is published (cover date April) featuring the first appearance of Batman's sidekick, Robin (Dick Grayson).
17	Major league baseball held a special spring training all-star game in Tampa, Florida to support the people of Finland. The exhibition raised more than $22,000 for the Finnish Relief Fund. The National League won the game 2-1 when Pete Coscarart of the Dodgers hit a walk-off single off Bob Feller in the bottom of the ninth.
23	Truth or Consequences, presented by Ralph Edwards, debuts on NBC Radio and is an instant hit with listeners. *Fun facts: Truth or Consequences became the first game show to air on broadcast television, airing as a one-time experiment on the first day of New York station WNBT's commercial program schedule on July 1, 1941. However, the series did not appear on TV again until 1950 when the medium had caught on commercially.*

	The 1940 and sixteenth U.S. Census is taken. *Census results: The population of the U.S. was determined to be 132,164,569, an increase of 7.3 percent over the 1930 population of 123,202,624 people - As of November 8, 2018, the U.S. is estimated to have a population of 328,953,020.*

April 7 - Booker T. Washington becomes the first African American to be depicted on a U.S. postage stamp. *Further information: Washington was from the last generation of black American leaders born into slavery and became the leading voice of the former slaves and their descendants. He was an educator, author, orator, and advisor to presidents, and between 1890 and 1915, was the dominant leader in the African-American community.*

10	President Franklin D. Roosevelt issued Executive Order 8389, freezing Danish and Norwegian assets in the United States so the Germans could not access them.
13	The New York Rangers win the Stanley Cup after defeating the Toronto Maple Leafs 4-2 in a best-of-seven final series. It is their third cup in 14 seasons of existence but it will be another 54 years before they win their fourth.
15	The opening day at Jamaica Racetrack in New York features its first use of pari-mutuel betting equipment - other NY tracks soon follow suit.

APR

21	Take It or Leave It, the forerunner to the popular quiz show The $64,000 Question, premieres on CBS radio with Bob Hawk as host.
23	A fire at the Rhythm Night Club in Natchez, Mississippi, kills 209. At the time this was the second deadliest building fire in the history of the nation.
24	Issue No.1 of the DC comic book Batman is published. This first issue marked the debut of the Joker and Catwoman (initially called The Cat). *Fun fact: A near mint copy (graded 9.2 grade by CGC) sold at auction for $567,625 in August 2013.*

MAY

10	President Roosevelt phones his Treasury Secretary Henry Morgenthau, Jr. and tells him to freeze Belgian, Dutch and Luxembourger assets to keep them out of Germany's hands after learning they had invaded France and the Low Countries at dawn.
16	President Roosevelt asks Congress for a $1.2 billion increase in defense spending to mobilize the Army and Navy and procure an additional 50,000 planes a year.
18	The 6.9Mw El Centro earthquake affects California's Imperial Valley with a maximum Mercalli intensity of X (Extreme). The earthquake causes nine deaths, twenty injuries and financial losses of around $6 million. Significant damage also occurs in Mexicali, Mexico.

May 25 - The Crypt of Civilization at Oglethorpe University in Brookhaven, Georgia is sealed. *Fun facts: The 2,000-cubic-foot (57-cubic-meter) room contains numerous artefacts and documents, and is designed for opening in the year 8113 AD. During the 50th anniversary year of its sealing, the Guinness Book of World Records cited the crypt as the "first successful attempt to bury a record of this culture for any future inhabitants or visitors to the planet Earth." Photo: An image of The Crypt and its creator, Oglethorpe University president Dr. Thornwell Jacobs.*

MAY

May 29 - The Vought XF4U-1, prototype of the F4U Corsair fighter aircraft, makes its first flight with Lyman A. Bullard, Jr. at the controls. *Fighter facts: The Corsair was designed and operated as a carrier-based aircraft, and entered service in large numbers with the U.S. Navy in late 1944 and early 1945. It quickly became one of the most capable carrier-based fighter-bombers of World War II. Extra: From the first prototype delivery to the U.S. Navy in 1940, to final delivery in 1953 to the French, 12,571 F4U Corsairs were manufactured in 16 separate models.*

JUN

3	The Supreme Court decided Minersville School District v. Gobitis, and ruled that public schools could compel students - in this case, Jehovah's Witnesses - to salute the American Flag and recite the Pledge of Allegiance despite the students' religious objections to these practices. The Supreme Court overruled this decision a mere three years later, in West Virginia State Board of Education v. Barnette.
10	President Roosevelt denounces Italy's actions with his "Stab in the Back" speech during a commencement address to the University of Virginia.
24	The Republican Party begins its national convention in Philadelphia and nominates Wendell Willkie as its candidate for president.

JUL

1	The doomed first Tacoma Narrows Bridge opens for business. At the time of its construction the bridge was the third longest suspension bridge in the world in terms of main span length, behind the Golden Gate Bridge and the George Washington Bridge. The bridge dramatically collapsed on November 7 during a 42mph wind storm killing Tubby, a black male cocker spaniel dog.

JUL

9	The Major League Baseball All-Star Game, the eighth playing of the mid-summer classic between the all-stars of the American League (AL) and National League (NL), was held at Sportsman's Park in St. Louis, Missouri, the home of the St. Louis Cardinals and St. Louis Browns. The game resulted in the National League defeating the American League 4-0.
18	Franklin D. Roosevelt was nominated almost unanimously at the Democratic National Convention to run for an unprecedented third term as President of the United States. Henry A. Wallace of Iowa was selected as his running mate.
19	The Two-Ocean Navy Act, also known as the Vinson-Walsh Act, was enacted. It was the largest naval procurement bill in U.S. history and increased the size of the Navy by 70%.
20	The Arroyo Seco Parkway, the first freeway in the Western United States, opens to traffic connecting downtown Los Angeles with Pasadena, California.
27	Billboard magazine begins publishing its top ten list of the best-selling retail records in the U.S. The first official No.1 single is "I'll Never Smile Again" by Tommy Dorsey and His Orchestra.

Bugs Bunny's evolution from 'Happy Rabbit' in 1938 to the present day.

27th July - Bugs Bunny makes his official debut in the Oscar-nominated cartoon short, A Wild Hare. *Fun facts: The prototypical version of Bugs Bunny appeared in four cartoons before making his official debut in 1940. Bugs Bunny has also appeared in more films than any other cartoon character and has his own star on the Hollywood Walk of Fame.*

AUG

4	General John J. Pershing, in a nationwide radio broadcast, urges all-out aid to Britain in order to defend the Americas. Meanwhile Charles Lindbergh speaks out to an isolationist rally at Soldier Field in Chicago.
15	The U.S. Army contracted with Chrysler to build the Detroit Arsenal Tank Plant in Warren, Michigan. It would be the first manufacturing plant ever built for the mass production of tanks in the U.S.
19	Gallup publishes the results of a poll asking Americans whether they approved of a proposal to sell 50 old destroyer ships to England - 62% approve of the idea, 38% disapprove.

AUG

23	The musical drama film Young People, starring 12-year-old Shirley Temple, premieres at the Roxy Theatre in New York City. This was Temple's final film for 20th Century Fox and it was thought at that time that it might be her last film ever. She actually went on to make 13 more movies, the last being A Kiss for Corliss (1949).

SEP

1	The New England hurricane reaches peak intensity as it passes by Cape Hatteras, North Carolina. The storm causes $4 million in damage and results in 7 fatalities.
2	An agreement between America and Great Britain is announced to the effect that 50 U.S. destroyers needed for escort work will be transferred to Great Britain. In return America gains 99-year leases on British bases in the North Atlantic, West Indies and Bermuda.
12	The Hercules Munitions Plant in Succasunna-Kenvil, New Jersey explodes killing 55 people. *Historical facts: The plant, one of several in northwest New Jersey, was founded in 1871 on 1,200 acres to provide dynamite to the local Iron Mines.*
16	The Selective Training and Service Act of 1940 is signed into law creating the first peacetime draft in U.S. history. The Act required that men who had reached their 21st birthday, but had not yet reached their 36th birthday, register with local draft boards.
23	Gallup publishes a poll asking, "Which of these two things do you think is the most important for the United States to try to do - to keep out of war ourselves or to help England win, even at the risk of getting into the war?" - 52% said help England, 48% said keep out.
26	The U.S. imposes a total embargo on all scrap metal shipments to Japan. The reasons were due to Japan's move into Indochina combined with its war with China, withdrawal from the League of Nations, alliance with Germany and Italy, and increasing militarization. The embargo hits Japan's economy particularly hard.

OCT

1	The first section of the Pennsylvania Turnpike, the country's first long-distance controlled-access highway, opens between Irwin and Carlisle. Homer D. Romberger, a feed and tallow driver from Carlisle, becomes the first motorist to enter the turnpike at Carlisle, and Carl A. Boe of McKeesport becomes the first motorist to enter at Irwin. *Turnpike facts: During its first 15 days of operation the road saw over 150,000 vehicles. By the end of its first year the road had earned $3 million in revenue from 5 million motorists, exceeding the $2.67 million needed for its operation and bond payments.*
1	Albert Einstein receives his final American citizenship papers (he took his citizenship test on June 22, 1940).
8	The Cincinnati Reds win a closely contested seven-game World Series 4-3 against the Detroit Tigers for their second championship, 21 years after their scandal-tainted victory against the Chicago White Sox in 1919.

OCT

21	The Ernest Hemingway novel For Whom the Bell Tolls is published. *Interesting facts: In 1941 the Pulitzer Prize committee for letters unanimously recommended For Whom the Bell Tolls be awarded the prize for that year. The Pulitzer Board agreed. However, Nicholas Murray Butler, president of Columbia University and ex officio head of the Pulitzer board at that time, found the novel offensive and persuaded the board to reverse its determination; no award was given for letters that year.*

NOV

5	Democrat incumbent Franklin D. Roosevelt defeats Republican challenger Wendell Willkie and becomes the nation's first and only third-term president; on November 7, 1944 Roosevelt became president for a fourth time when he defeated Republican Thomas E. Dewey.
8	The 5,883-ton American steamship City of Rayville is hit a German naval mine and sinks in the Bass Strait off Cape Otway, Australia. The 38 crew members were able to safely abandon the vessel in lifeboats, although one mariner (James Bryan of Norfolk, Virginia) re-entered the vessel to find personal items and subsequently drowned. The vessel sank, bow first, in 35 minutes. It is the first U.S. vessel to be lost during World War II.
10	The Copacabana nightclub opens in New York City. *Fun facts: Many entertainers such as Danny Thomas, Pat Cooper, and the comedy team of Dean Martin and Jerry Lewis made their New York debuts at the Copacabana. Extra: The Barry Manilow song 'Copacabana' (1978), the third and final single from Manilow's fifth studio album, was named after the club.*

November 11 - Armistice Day Blizzard: An intense early-season winter storm cuts a 1,000-mile-wide swath through the middle of the country from Kansas to Michigan killing 144 people. Snowfalls of up to 27 inches, winds of 50 to 80mph, 20-foot snow drifts, and 50-degree Fahrenheit temperature drops were common over parts of the states of Nebraska, South Dakota, Iowa, Minnesota, Wisconsin, and Michigan. *Interesting fact: The Armistice Day Blizzard ranks as No.2 in Minnesota's list of the top five weather events of the 20th century.*

NOV

13	Walt Disney's Fantasia is released. It is the first box office failure for Disney, though it recoups its cost years later and becomes one of the most highly regarded of Disney's films.
15	The comedy team of Abbott and Costello make their screen debut in the comedy film One Night In The Tropics. *Fun facts: Although they are listed as supporting actors, they steal the picture with five of their classic routines, including an abbreviated version of "Who's On First?" Their work earns them a two-picture deal with Universal, and their next film, Buck Privates, makes them bona fide movie stars.*
16	An unexploded pipe bomb is found in the Consolidated Edison office building. *Follow up: This was the first of at least 33 bombs, of which 22 exploded injuring 15 people, planted by the electrician and mechanic George Metesky. Known as the Mad Bomber he was eventually apprehended in January 1957, found legally insane and committed to a state mental hospital. He was released from the hospital in 1973, and died 20 years later in 1993 aged 90.*

DEC

December 8 - The Chicago Bears beat the Washington Redskins 73-0 in the NFL Championship Game at Griffith Stadium in Washington, D.C. It remains the most lopsided victory in NFL history.

10	The 1941 NFL draft is held at the Willard Hotel in Washington D.C. The Chicago Bears select Tom Harmon of the University of Michigan as the No.1 overall pick.
20	A 5.6Mw earthquake shakes New Hampshire with a maximum Mercalli intensity of VII (Very strong). This earthquake is followed four days later by another 5.6Mw shock. The total damage from both events is light.
29	President Roosevelt, in a fireside chat to the nation, declares that the U.S. must become "the great arsenal of democracy."

1. January 2: The Irish government introduces emergency powers to extend the power of internment from foreign nationals to Irish citizens, and to allow juryless court martials of civilians. These were in response to increased activity by the Irish Republican Army (IRA).

2. January 8: Food rationing is introduced in the United Kingdom for bacon, butter and sugar. Successive ration schemes follow for meat, tea, jelly, biscuits, breakfast cereals, cheese, eggs, lard, milk, and canned and dried fruit.

3. March: Otto Frisch and Rudolf Peierls, at this time working at the University of Birmingham, England, calculate that an atomic bomb could be produced using very much less enriched uranium than had previously been supposed, making it a practical proposition. It helped send both Britain and America down a path which led to the MAUD Committee, the Tube Alloys project, the Manhattan Project, and ultimately the atomic bombings of Hiroshima and Nagasaki.

4. March 3-9: The 83,673-ton RMS Queen Elizabeth makes her secret maiden voyage from Clydebank, Scotland to New York. Captain John Townley zigzagged across the Atlantic to elude German U-Boats, taking six days at an average speed of 26 knots. After his arrival in New York Captain Townley received two telegrams, one from his wife congratulating him and the other from Her Majesty Queen Elizabeth thanking him for the vessel's safe delivery. *Interesting facts: During her WWII service as a troopship RMS Queen Elizabeth carried more than 750,000 troops and sailed some 500,000 miles.*

5. March 18: Hitler meets with Mussolini at the Brenner Pass in the Alps. Hitler makes it clear that German troops are poised to launch an offensive in the west and that Mussolini would have to decide whether Italy would join in the attack or not. Since Italy was still not ready for war, Mussolini suggested that the offensive could be delayed a few more months, to which Hitler replied that Germany was not altering its plans to suit Italy. The two agreed that Italy would come into the war in due course.

6. March 20: The entire French cabinet resign. Although Prime Minister Édouard Daladier had won a vote of confidence in the Chamber of Deputies 239-1, there were so many abstentions among the 551 members that he recognized the vote as a defeat.

7. March 26: A federal election is held in Canada and the Liberal government of William Lyon Mackenzie King is re-elected to another majority government.

8. April 9: At 5:20am in Norway (4:20am in Denmark), the German envoys in Oslo and Copenhagen presented the Norwegian and Danish governments with a German ultimatum demanding that they immediately accept the "protection of the Reich." Denmark capitulated so as to not provoke mass bloodshed at the hands of the Germans, and the country was invaded in six hours. Norwegian Foreign Affairs Minister Halvdan Koht, however, responded with the defiant words "Vi gir oss ikke frivillig, kampen er allerede i gang" ("We will not submit voluntarily; the struggle is already underway"). The entire Norwegian government including King Haakon VII fled the capital that morning for the mountains in the north.

9. April 29: Helsinki forfeits the 1940 Summer Olympics and just a week later (on May 6) the International Olympic Committee formally cancels them. The Olympics would not resume again until the London Games in 1948.

10.	May 10: Neville Chamberlain goes to Buckingham Palace at around 6pm and resigns as Prime Minister of the United Kingdom. King George VI asks Winston Churchill to form the next government and Churchill accepts.
11.	May 13-14: Queen Wilhelmina of the Netherlands and her government are evacuated to London, using Royal Navy destroyer HMS Hereward, following the German invasion of the Low Countries.

12. May 26 - June 4: The Dunkirk evacuation of the British Expeditionary Force, code-named Operation Dynamo (also known as the Miracle of Dunkirk), takes place from the beaches and harbour of Dunkirk, in the north of France. The operation commenced after large numbers of Belgian, British and French troops were cut off and surrounded by German troops during the six-week long Battle of France. In a speech to the House of Commons, Prime Minister Winston Churchill called this "a colossal military disaster", saying "the whole root and core and brain of the British Army" had been stranded at Dunkirk and seemed about to perish or be captured. Later in his "we shall fight on the beaches" speech on June 4, he hailed their rescue as a "miracle of deliverance". *Dunkirk evacuation facts: On the first day only 7,669 Allied soldiers were evacuated, but by the end of the eighth day, 338,226 of them had been rescued by a hastily assembled fleet of 861 British and Allied ships (243 of which were sunk during the evacuation). Many troops were able to embark from the harbour's protective mole onto 39 Royal Navy destroyers, four Royal Canadian Navy destroyers, and a variety of civilian merchant ships, while others had to wade out from the beaches, waiting for hours in shoulder-deep water. The BEF lost 68,000 soldiers during the French campaign and had to abandon nearly all of its tanks, vehicles, and equipment. Churchill reminded the country that "we must be very careful not to assign to this deliverance the attributes of a victory. Wars are not won by evacuations."*

13.	June 10: At 6pm Benito Mussolini appeared on the balcony of the Palazzo Venezia to announce that in six hours Italy would be in a state of war with France and Britain.

14.	June 10: Norway surrenders to Germany; King Haakon VII and his cabinet had escaped to London three days previously to form a government in exile.
15.	June 17: RMS Lancastria, serving as a troopship, is bombed and sunk by the Luftwaffe while evacuating British troops and nationals from Saint-Nazaire, France, with the loss of at least 4,000 lives. This is the largest single-ship loss of life in British maritime history; the immense loss of life was such that the British government suppressed news of the disaster - the story was eventually broken on the July 25 in the U.S. by The New York Times, and in Britain by The Scotsman on July 26, more than five weeks after the sinking.
16.	June 18: Churchill makes his "This was their finest hour" speech to the House of Commons. It was the third of three speeches which he gave during the period of the Battle of France, and one of the great rallying cries in world history.
17.	June 18: General Charles de Gaulle, de facto leader of the Free French Forces, makes his first broadcast appeal over Radio Londres, from London, rallying French Resistance.
18.	July 2: The passenger ship Arandora Star, carrying civilian internees and POWs of Italian and German origin from Liverpool, England to Canada, is torpedoed and sunk by German submarine U-47 off northwest Ireland with the loss of 865 lives.
19.	August 20: Howard Florey and a team including Ernst Chain at the Sir William Dunn School of Pathology, University of Oxford, England, publish their laboratory results showing the in vivo bactericidal action of penicillin.
20.	August 25: The British RAF bomb Berlin for the first time. Ninety-five aircraft were dispatched to bomb Tempelhof Airport near the center of Berlin and Siemensstadt, of which 81 dropped their bombs in and around Berlin. While the damage was slight the psychological effect on Hitler was greater. This prompted Hitler to order the shift of the Luftwaffe's target from British airfields and air defences to British cities.
21.	September 12: Prehistoric cave paintings are discovered in the Lascaux Cave near Montignac, France by 18-year-old Marcel Ravidat. The paintings are mostly of animals and are some of the finest examples of art from the Upper Paleolithic age. *Follow up: The cave complex was opened to the public on July 14, 1948 but by 1955, carbon dioxide, heat, humidity, and other contaminants produced by 1,200 visitors per day had visibly damaged the paintings. As air condition deteriorated, fungi and lichen increasingly infested the walls, and as a consequence, the cave was eventually closed to the public in 1963.*
22.	September 15: British RAF command claims victory over the Luftwaffe in the Battle of Britain; this day has since been known as "Battle of Britain Day".
23.	November 2: In one of the most extraordinary aviation incidents of the war, Greek Air Force pilot Marinos Mitralexis, after running out of ammunition, brings down and Italian bomber by ramming its rudder and sending it out of control. He then makes an emergency landing near the crashed bomber. Having landed, Mitralexis proceeds to arrest the four surviving crew members of the enemy aircraft, who had parachuted to safety, using his pistol. *Bravery: For this extraordinary feat, Mitralexis was promoted and awarded a number of medals, including Greece's highest award for bravery, the Gold Cross of Valour.*
24.	November 25: The de Havilland Mosquito makes its first flight. The British twin-engine combat aircraft was unusual in that its frame was constructed almost entirely of wood. *Fun fact: It was nicknamed The Wooden Wonder, or "Mossie" to its crews.*
25.	December 24: An unofficial two-day Christmas truce begins in the aerial war between Britain and Germany.

THE BLITZ

The Blitz began on September 7 when 350 bombers dropped 300 tonnes of bombs on the docks and streets of the East End of London, England. London was then systematically bombed by the Luftwaffe for 56 out of the following 57 days and nights. *London Blitz facts: London was targeted a total of 71 times by the Luftwaffe's bombing campaign during the Blitz. During these raids 32,000 civilians in London were killed and 87,000 were seriously injured.*

BIRTHS
U.S. PERSONALITIES
BORN IN 1940

Carol Elizabeth Heiss Jenkins

b. January 20, 1940

Figure skater who first came to national prominence in 1951 when she won the U.S. novice ladies' title at age 11, and in 1953 when she became the first female skater to land a double axel jump. Her career achievements include being the 1960 Olympic champion, the 1956 Olympic silver medalist, and a five-time World champion (1956-1960). In 1976 Heiss was inducted into the World Figure Skating Hall of Fame and the United States Figure Skating Hall of Fame.

Jack William Nicklaus

b. January 21, 1940

Professional golfer, nicknamed 'The Golden Bear', whom many observers regard as the greatest golfer of all time. During his career he won a record 18 major championships, while producing 19 second-place and 9 third-place finishes. Although he focused on the majors, and played only a selective schedule of regular PGA Tour events, he still finished with 73 victories, third on the all-time list behind Sam Snead (82) and Tiger Woods (80). Nicklaus was inducted into the World Golf Hall of Fame's inaugural class of 1974.

Francis Asbury Tarkenton

b. February 3, 1940

NFL quarterback, television personality, and computer software executive. Tarkenton played in the NFL for 18 seasons; 13 seasons with the Minnesota Vikings and 5 with the New York Giants. At the time of his retirement he owned every major quarterback record. He was inducted into the Pro Football Hall of Fame in 1986 and the College Football Hall of Fame in 1987, and in 1999 was ranked No.59 on The Sporting News list of the 100 Greatest Football Players.

George Andrew Romero

b. February 4, 1940
d. July 16, 2017

American-Canadian filmmaker, writer and editor. He is best known for his series horror films about an imagined zombie apocalypse, beginning with Night Of The Living Dead (1968), and continuing with Dawn Of The Dead (1978) and Day Of The Dead (1985). Aside from this series he has made a number of other notable movies as well as the 1983-1988 television series Tales From The Darkside. Romero is often noted as an influential pioneer of the horror-film genre and has been called an the 'Father of the Zombie Film'.

Gene Francis Alan Pitney

b. February 17, 1940
d. April 5, 2006

Singer-songwriter, musician and sound engineer who charted a total of 16 Top 40 hits in the United States, and 22 in the United Kingdom. He also wrote the early 1960s hits Rubber Ball recorded by Bobby Vee, He's A Rebel by the Crystals, and Hello Mary Lou by Ricky Nelson. His own best-selling records include 24 Hours From Tulsa, Town Without Pity, and the British No.1 Something's Gotten Hold Of My Heart. Pitney was inducted into the Rock and Roll Hall of Fame in 2002.

William 'Smokey' Robinson Jr.

b. February 19, 1940

Singer, songwriter, record producer, and former record executive. He was the founder and frontman of the Motown vocal group the Miracles, for which he was also chief songwriter and producer. He led the group from its 1955 origins until 1972 when he announced a retirement to focus on his role as Motown's vice president - a year later he returned to the music industry as a solo artist. Robinson was inducted into the Rock and Roll Hall of Fame in 1987 and in 2016 was awarded the Library of Congress Gershwin Prize.

Peter Henry Fonda

b. February 23, 1940

Actor who is the son of Henry Fonda and younger brother of Jane Fonda. He is known as a counterculture icon of the 1960s and the star of films such as The Wild Angels (1966), Easy Rider (1969) and Ulee's Gold (1997). He has been twice nominated for Academy Awards; for Best Original Screenplay with Easy Rider and Best Actor for Ulee's Gold - for the latter, he won the Golden Globe Award for Best Actor. Fonda also won the Golden Globe Award for Best Supporting Actor for The Passion of Ayn Rand (1999).

Ronald Edward Santo

b. February 25, 1940
d. December 3, 2010

A MLB third baseman who played for the Chicago Cubs from 1960 through 1973, and the Chicago White Sox in 1974. Santo was an All-Star for nine seasons during his 15-year career and is the only third baseman in MLB history to post eight consecutive seasons with over 90 runs batted in (RBI) (1963-1970). He was also a Gold Glove Award winner for five consecutive seasons and was posthumously inducted into the National Baseball Hall of Fame in 2012.

Mario Gabriele Andretti

b. February 28, 1940

One of the most successful American racing drivers in the history of the sport. He is one of only two drivers to have won races in Formula One, IndyCar, World Sportscar Championship and NASCAR (the other being Dan Gurney). He has also won races in midget cars, and sprint cars. During his career Andretti won the 1978 Formula One World Championship, four IndyCar titles (three under USAC-sanctioning, one under CART), and IROC VI.

Carlos Ray Norris

b. March 10, 1940

Martial artist, actor, film producer and screenwriter. After serving in the U.S. Air Force he competed as a martial artist and in 1968 became the Professional Middleweight Karate Champion (a title he held for six consecutive years). He has appeared in a number of action films, including Way Of The Dragon (1972) alongside Bruce Lee, and on television he played the title role in Walker, Texas Ranger (1993-2001). Norris has also written several books and has twice been a New York Times best-selling author.

Nancy Patricia Pelosi
(née D'Alesandro)

b. March 26, 1940

Politician who has twice served as Speaker of the U.S. House of Representatives. She is not only the only woman to have served as Speaker, but is also the highest-ranking elected woman in United States history - she is second in the presidential line of succession immediately after the vice president. Pelosi has led House Democrats since 2003 (the first woman to lead a party in Congress) and is in her 17th term as a congresswoman.

John Joseph 'Hondo' Havlicek

b. April 8, 1940

Professional basketball player who competed for 16 seasons with the Boston Celtics, winning eight NBA championships, four of them coming in his first four seasons. In the NBA only teammates Bill Russell and Sam Jones have won more championships during their playing careers. Havlicek is widely considered to be one of the greatest players in the history of the game and was inducted as a member of the Naismith Memorial Basketball Hall of Fame in 1984.

Alfredo James Pacino

b. April 25, 1940

Actor and filmmaker whose career has spanned more than five decades. He achieved international acclaim and recognition for his breakthrough role as Michael Corleone in Francis Ford Coppola's The Godfather (1972), reprising the role in the equally successful sequels The Godfather Part II (1974) and The Godfather Part III (1990). Pacino is one of just a few performers to have won a competitive Oscar, an Emmy, and a Tony Award for acting, dubbed the 'Triple Crown of Acting'.

Eric Hilliard 'Ricky' Nelson

b. May 8, 1940
d. December 31, 1985

Rock and roll star, musician, and singer-songwriter. From age eight he starred alongside his family in the radio and television series The Adventures of Ozzie and Harriet. In 1957 he began a long and successful career as a popular recording artist, placing 53 songs in the charts between 1957 and 1973; his first No.1 single, Poor Little Fool (1958), was the very first song to top Billboard magazine's newly created Hot 100 chart. Nelson was inducted into the Rock and Roll Hall of Fame in 1987.

Nancy Sandra Sinatra

b. June 8, 1940

Singer and actress who is the eldest daughter of Frank and Nancy (Barbato) Sinatra and is widely known for her 1966 signature hit These Boots Are Made For Walkin'. Other notable recordings include Sugar Town (1966), the 1967 No.1 Somethin' Stupid (a duet with her father), and her cover of Cher's Bang Bang (My Baby Shot Me Down). Sinatra also had a brief acting career in the mid-1960s which included co-starring with Elvis Presley in the movie Speedway (1968).

Shirley Muldowney

b. June 19, 1940

Auto racer known professionally as 'Cha Cha' and the 'First Lady of Drag Racing'. She was the first woman to receive a license from the National Hot Rod Association (NHRA) to drive a Top Fuel dragster. She won the NHRA Top Fuel championship in 1977, 1980 and 1982, becoming the first person to win two and three Top Fuel titles. Muldowney was inducted into the Motorsports Hall of Fame of America in 1990, and the International Motorsports Hall of Fame in 2004.

Wilma Glodean Rudolph

b. June 23, 1940
d. November 12, 1994

Sprinter who became a world-record-holding Olympic champion and international sports icon in track and field, following her successes in the 1956 and 1960 Olympic Games. She was acclaimed the fastest woman in the world in the 1960s and became the first American woman to win three gold medals in a single Olympic Games. Rudolph became a role model for black and female athletes and her successes helped elevate women's track and field in the United States.

George Alexander 'Alex' Trebek

b. July 22, 1940

Canadian-American television personality who has been the host of the syndicated game show Jeopardy! since it was revived in 1984, and has also hosted a number of other game shows, including The Wizard of Odds, Double Dare, High Rollers, Battlestars, Classic Concentration, and To Tell the Truth. A native of Canada, he became a naturalized United States citizen in 1998. On October 31, 2018, Trebek signed a contract to continue to host Jeopardy! until 2022.

Ramón Gerard Antonio Estévez

b. August 3, 1940

Actor, known professionally as Martin Sheen, who first became known for his roles in the films The Subject Was Roses (1968) and Badlands (1973). He later achieved wide recognition for his leading role in Apocalypse Now (1979) and as President Josiah Bartlet in the television series The West Wing (1999-2006). In his acting career, Sheen has been nominated for ten Emmy Awards (winning one) and has also earned eight nominations for Golden Globe Awards.

Raquel Welch

b. September 5, 1940

Actress and singer who first won attention for her role as Cora Peterson in Fantastic Voyage (1966). It was though as Loana in the film One Million Years B.C. (1966) that turned her into an international celebrity and sex symbol. She later starred in other notable films including Bedazzled (1967), Bandolero! (1968), 100 Rifles (1969) and Myra Breckinridge (1970). Welch's unique persona on film made her into an icon of the 1960s and 1970s, portraying strong female characters and breaking the mold of the submissive sex symbol.

Frankie Avalon

b. September 18, 1940

Actor, singer and former teen idol who had 31 charted U.S. Billboard singles from 1958 to late 1962, including two No.1 hits, Venus, and Why, in 1959. In the early 1960s he began taking small parts in movies, most notably in John Wayne's The Alamo (1960). His first starring role was in Drums Of Africa (1963) but it was when he was paired with former Mouseketeer Annette Funicello in Beach Party (1963), and its sequels, that his movie career really took off.

David Albert DeBusschere

b. October 16, 1940
d. May 14, 2003

Professional NBA player and coach, and MLB player (one of only 13 athletes to have played in both leagues). As a basketball player he was renowned for his physical style of play and tenacious defense. During his 12-year career (1962-1974) he averaged 16.1 points and 11 rebounds per game while being named to eight NBA All-Star teams. DeBusschere was elected to the Naismith Memorial Basketball Hall of Fame in 1983 and in 1996, was named as one of the 50 greatest players in NBA history.

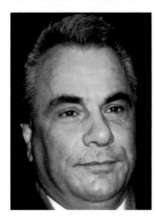

John Joseph Gotti Jr.

b. October 27, 1940
d. June 10, 2002

Italian-American gangster who became boss of the Gambino crime family in New York City. He grew up in poverty and turned to a life of crime at an early age. Gotti quickly rose to prominence becoming one of the crime family's biggest earners and a protégé of Gambino family underboss Aniello Dellacroce. At his peak he was one of the most powerful and dangerous crime bosses in the country. Gotti was sentenced to life in prison without parole for his crimes in 1992.

Lee Jun-fan

b. November 27, 1940
d. July 20, 1973

Actor, director, martial artist, martial arts instructor and philosopher known professionally as Bruce Lee. He instructed several World Karate Champions including Chuck Norris, Joe Lewis and Mike Stone. Between the three of them, during their training with Lee, they won every karate championship in the United States. Lee was the founder of the martial art Jeet Kune Do and is considered by commentators, critics, media, and other martial artists to be one of the most influential martial artists of the 20th century.

Richard Franklin Lennox Thomas Pryor

b. December 1, 1940
d. December 10, 2005

Stand-up comedian, actor and social critic. Known for uncompromising examinations of racism and topical contemporary issues, he reached a broad audience with his trenchant observations and storytelling style, and is widely regarded as one of the greatest and most influential stand-up comedians of all time. Pryor is the winner of an Emmy Award (1973), five Grammy Awards (1974/1975/1976/1981/1982), the Writers Guild of America Award (1974), and the first-ever Kennedy Center Mark Twain Prize for American Humor (1998).

Marie Dionne Warwick

b. December 12, 1940

Singer, actress and television show host who became a United Nations Global Ambassador for the Food and Agriculture Organization, and a United States Ambassador of Health. Warwick ranks among the 40 biggest hit makers of the entire rock era and is second only to Aretha Franklin as the most-charted female vocalist of all time; between 1962 and 1998, 56 of her singles made the Billboard Hot 100 Chart (80 if you include all Billboard charts combined).

Frank Vincent Zappa

b. December 21, 1940
d. December 4, 1993

Musician, composer, activist and filmmaker whose career spanned more than 30 years. Zappa composed rock, pop, jazz, jazz fusion, orchestral and musique concrète works, and produced almost all of his 60-plus albums. He is considered one of the most innovative and stylistically diverse rock musicians of his era. His honors include his 1995 induction into the Rock and Roll Hall of Fame and the 1997 Grammy Lifetime Achievement Award.

NOTABLE DEATHS

Jan 4	Flora Finch (b. June 17, 1867) - English-born vaudevillian and actress who starred in over 300 silent films.
Jan 19	William Edgar Borah (b. June 29, 1865) - Outspoken Republican Senator (1907-1940) who is one of the best-known figures in Idaho's history.
Feb 1	Philip Francis Nowlan (b. November 13, 1888) - Science fiction author best known as the creator of Buck Rogers.
Feb 4	Samuel Matthews Vauclain (b. May 18, 1856) - Engineer and inventor of the Vauclain compound locomotive.
Feb 9	William Edward Dodd (b. October 21, 1869) - Historian, author and diplomat who served as the United States Ambassador to Germany from 1933 to 1937.
Apr 26	Henry Ossian Flipper (b. March 21, 1856) - Soldier and former slave who in 1877 became the first African American to graduate from the Military Academy at West Point.
Jun 21	Smedley Darlington Butler (b. July 30, 1881) - Marine Corps major general who at the time of his death was the most decorated Marine in U.S. history.
Jun 21	John Taliaferro Thompson (b. December 31, 1860) - Army officer best remembered as the inventor of the Thompson submachine gun.
Jul 1	Bernard 'Ben' Turpin (b. September 19, 1869) - Comedian and actor best remembered for his work in silent films.
Jul 15	Robert Pershing Wadlow (b. February 22, 1918) - The world's tallest person at 8ft 11.1in; also known as the Alton Giant and the Giant of Illinois.
Aug 5	Frederick Albert Cook (b. June 10, 1865) - Explorer, physician and ethnographer noted for his claim (unproven) of having reached the North Pole on April 21, 1908.
Aug 8	Johnny Dodds (b. April 12, 1892) - Jazz clarinetist and alto saxophonist best known for his recordings under his own name and with bands such as those of Joe 'King' Oliver, Jelly Roll Morton, Lovie Austin and Louis Armstrong.
Aug 13	George C. Pearce (b. June 26, 1865) - Film actor, primarily of the silent era, who appeared in 133 films between 1914 and 1939.
Aug 17	William Meade Lindsley Fiske III (b. June 4, 1911) - The 1928 and 1932 Olympic champion bobsled driver; he was one of the first American pilots killed in action in World War II.
Aug 18	Walter Percy Chrysler (b. April 2, 1875) - Automotive industry executive and founder of Chrysler Corporation.
Aug 21	Ernest Lawrence Thayer (b. August 14, 1863) - Writer and poet who wrote the poem Casey (or Casey at the Bat), one of the best-known poems in American literature.
Sep 1	Lillian D. Wald (b. March 10, 1867) - Nurse, humanitarian and author who was known for her contributions to human rights, and was the founder of American community nursing.
Sep 10	Edward LeSaint (b. December 13, 1870) - Actor and director who appeared in over 300 films, and directed more than 90.
Sep 25	Helen Marguerite Clark (b. February 22, 1883) - Stage and silent film actress who at one time was second only to Mary Pickford in popularity.
Oct 12	Thomas Edwin Mix (b. January 6, 1880) - Film actor who was Hollywood's first Western star in the early days of the cinema.

Nov 17	Raymond Pearl (b. 3 June 1879) - Biologist, regarded as one of the founders of biogerontology.
Dec 15	William Robert 'Sliding Billy' Hamilton (b. February 16, 1866) - 19th century Major League Baseball player who was elected to the National Baseball Hall of Fame and Museum in 1961.
Dec 21	Francis Scott Key Fitzgerald (b. September 24, 1896) - Fiction writer whose works helped to illustrate the flamboyance and excess of the Jazz Age.
Dec 22	Nathanael West (b. October 17, 1903) - Author and screenwriter remembered for his two darkly satirical novels: Miss Lonelyhearts (1933) and The Day Of The Locust (1939).
Dec 23	Eddie August Henry Schneider (b. October 20, 1911) - Aviator who set three transcontinental airspeed records for pilots under the age of 21 (1930).
Dec 25	Agnes Ayres (b. April 4, 1898) - Actress who rose to fame during the silent film era and was probably best known for her role as Lady Diana Mayo in The Sheik (1921) opposite Rudolph Valentino.
Dec 26	Daniel Frohman (b. August 22, 1851) - Theatrical producer and manager, and an early film producer.

Actresses Maureen O'Sullivan and Ann Morris stand next to giant Robert Wadlow. Wadlow was 8ft 8½in tall at the time this photo was taken.

POPULAR MUSIC

Glenn Miller	No.1	In The Mood
Artie Shaw	No.2	Frenesi
Tommy Dorsey & Frank Sinatra	No.3	I'll Never Smile Again
Cliff Edwards (Ukelele Ike)	No.4	When You Wish Upon A Star
Bing Crosby	No.5	Only Forever
The Ink Spots	No.6	Whispering Grass
Jimmy Dorsey	No.7	The Breeze And I
Jimmie Davis	No.8	You Are My Sunshine
Bob Wills & His Texas Playboys	No.9	New San Antonio Rose
The Andrews Sisters	No.10	Ferryboat Serenade

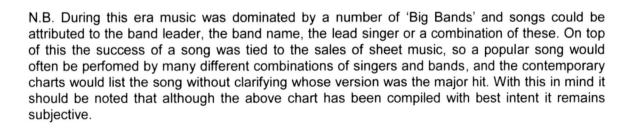

N.B. During this era music was dominated by a number of 'Big Bands' and songs could be attributed to the band leader, the band name, the lead singer or a combination of these. On top of this the success of a song was tied to the sales of sheet music, so a popular song would often be perfomed by many different combinations of singers and bands, and the contemporary charts would list the song without clarifying whose version was the major hit. With this in mind it should be noted that although the above chart has been compiled with best intent it remains subjective.

Glenn Miller
In The Mood

Label:	Written by:	Length:
His Master's Voice	Razaf / Garland	3 mins 29 secs

Alton Glenn Miller (b. March 1, 1904 - MIA December 15, 1944) was a big-band musician, arranger, composer and bandleader in the swing era. He was the best-selling recording artist from 1939 to 1943, leading one of the best-known big bands and scoring 23 No.1 hits. In The Mood became an anthem of the times and sold over 60 million records, the most of any swing band. In 1983 the song was inducted into the Grammy Hall of Fame and 2004 into the Library of Congress National Recording Registry.

Artie Shaw
Frenesi

Label:	Written by:	Length:
Victor	Alberto Dominguez	3 mins

Artie Shaw (b. Arthur Jacob Arshawsky; May 23, 1910 - d. December 30, 2004) was a clarinetist, composer, bandleader, author and actor. Widely regarded as one of jazz's finest clarinetists, he led one of the most popular big bands of the late 1930s through the early 1940s. Shaw's Frenesi was inducted into the Grammy Hall of Fame in 1982.

Tommy Dorsey & Frank Sinatra
I'll Never Smile Again

Label:	Written by:	Length:
Victor	Ruth Lowe	3 mins 12 secs

I'll Never Smile Again was recorded by jazz trombonist, composer, conductor and bandleader Tommy Dorsey (b. November 19, 1905 - d. November 26, 1956) and His Orchestra, with vocals provided by Frank Sinatra (b. December 12, 1915 - d. May 14, 1998) and The Pied Pipers. This was Dorsey's biggest hit single and was the first No.1 on Billboard's first official national music chart, staying at the top spot for 12 weeks. The tune was inducted into the Grammy Hall of Fame in 1982.

Cliff Edwards (Ukelele Ike)
When You Wish Upon A Star

Label:	Written by:	Length:
Decca	Harline / Washington	3 mins 17 secs

Clifton Avon Edwards (b. June 14, 1895 - d. July 17, 1971) was a musician, singer, actor and voice actor, otherwise known as 'Ukulele Ike', who enjoyed considerable popularity in the 1920s and early 1930s. When You Wish Upon a Star was written for Walt Disney's 1940 adaptation of Pinocchio and was sung by Edwards in the character of Jiminy Cricket. The song won the 1940 Academy Award for Best Original Song and was inducted into the Grammy Hall of Fame in 2002.

5 Bing Crosby
Only Forever

Label:	Written by:	Length:
Decca	Monaco / Burke	3 mins 12 secs

Harry Lillis 'Bing' Crosby, Jr. (b. May 3, 1903 - d. October 14, 1977) was a singer and actor. Crosby's trademark warm bass-baritone voice made him the best-selling recording artist of the 20th century selling close to a billion records, tapes, compact discs and digital downloads worldwide. Only Forever was written by James V. Monaco and Johnny Burke for the 1940 film Rhythm On The River, and was nominated for the Academy Award for Best Original Song.

---

6 The Ink Spots
Whispering Grass

Label:	Written by:	Length:
Decca	Fred & Doris Fisher	2 mins 39 secs

The Ink Spots, Bill Kenny (b. June 12, 1914 - d. March 23, 1978), Deek Watson (b. July 18, 1909 - d. November 4, 1969), Charlie Fuqua (b. October 20, 1910 - d. December 21, 1971), and Hoppy Jones (b. February 17, 1905 - d. October 18, 1944), were a pop vocal group who gained international fame in the 1930s and 1940s. In 1989 the Ink Spots were inducted into the Rock and Roll Hall of Fame, and in 1999 they were inducted into the Vocal Group Hall of Fame.

7 Jimmy Dorsey
The Breeze And I

Label:	Written by:	Length:
Decca	Stillman / Camarata	2 mins 55 secs

James Dorsey (b. February 29, 1904 - d. June 12, 1957) was jazz clarinetist, saxophonist, composer and big band leader, who was known as 'JD'. He recorded and composed the jazz and pop standards I'm Glad There Is You (In This World Of Ordinary People) and It's The Dreamer In Me. The Breeze And I featured big band vocalist Bob Eberly (b. July 24, 1916 - d. November 17, 1981) and was originally written by the Cuban composer Ernesto Lecuona as part of his suite Andalucía in 1928.

8 Jimmie Davis
You Are My Sunshine

Label:	Written by:	Length:
Decca	Davis / Mitchell	3 mins 42 secs

James Houston Davis (b. September 11, 1899 - d. November 5, 2000) was a singer and songwriter, as well as a politician and former governor of Louisiana (1944-1948 and 1960-1964). He was a nationally popular country music and gospel singer from the 1930s into the 1960s, occasionally recording and performing as late as the early 1990s. He appeared as himself in a number of Hollywood movies and has been inducted into the Country Music Hall of Fame and the Southern Gospel Music Association Hall of Fame. You Are My Sunshine has been covered numerous times - so often in fact, that it is one of the most commercially programmed numbers in American popular music.

Bob Wills & His Texas Playboys
New San Antonio Rose

Label:	Written by:	Length:
Okeh	Bob Wills	3 mins 25 secs

James Robert Wills (b. March 6, 1905 - d. May 13, 1975) was a musician, songwriter and bandleader who is considered by music authorities as the co-founder of Western swing. San Antonio Rose was the signature song of Bob Wills and His Texas Playboys. It was originally an instrumental song written by Wills, but band members added lyrics and it was retitled "New San Antonio Rose". Wills and the Texas Playboys were inducted into The Rock and Roll Hall of Fame in 1999.

The Andrews Sisters
Ferryboat Serenade

Label:	Written by:	Length:
Decca	Lazzaro / Adamson / Panzeri	2 mins 57 secs

The Andrews Sisters were a close harmony singing group from the eras of swing and boogie-woogie. The group consisted of three sisters: LaVerne Sophia (b. July 6, 1911 - d. May 8, 1967), Maxene Angelyn (b. January 3, 1916 - d. October 21, 1995) and Patricia Marie (b. February 16, 1918 - d. January 30, 2013). Throughout their long career the sisters sold well over 75 million records.

1940: TOP FILMS

1. **Rebecca** - *United Artists*
2. **The Philadelphia Story** - *MGM*
3. **The Grapes Of Wrath** - *20ᵗʰ Century-Fox*
4. **The Great Dictator** - *United Artists*
5. **Pinocchio** - *Disney*

OSCARS

Best Picture: Rebecca
Most Nominations: Rebecca (11)
Most Wins: The Thief of Bagdad (3)

Photo 1: James Stewart and Ginger Rogers with their Oscars for best actor and actress.
Photo 2: Alfred Lunt and Lynn Fontanne congratulating Jane Darwell (center right) and Walter Brennan (far right) for their Academy Award wins.

Best Director: John Ford - *The Grapes of Wrath*

Best Actor: James Stewart - *The Philadelphia Story*
Best Actress: Ginger Rogers - *Kitty Foyle*
Best Supporting Actor: Walter Brennan - *The Westerner*
Best Supporting Actress: Jane Darwell - *The Grapes of Wrath*

The 13ᵗʰ Academy Awards were presented on February 27, 1941.

REBECCA

Directed by: Alfred Hitchcock - Runtime: 2 hours 10 minutes

Maxim de Winter, still troubled by the death of his first wife Rebecca, falls in love with a shy ladies' companion. They get married but the second Mrs. de Winter soon discovers that Rebecca still has a strange hold on everyone in the house…

STARRING

Laurence Olivier
Born: May 22, 1907
Died: July 11, 1989

Character:
Maxim de Winter

Actor and director who, along with his contemporaries Ralph Richardson, Peggy Ashcroft and John Gielgud, dominated the British stage of the mid-20th century. He also worked in films throughout his career and received four Academy Awards, two British Academy Film Awards, five Emmy Awards and three Golden Globe Awards. He is commemorated today in the Laurence Olivier Awards, given annually by the Society of London Theatre.

Joan Fontaine
Born: October 22, 1917
Died: December 15, 2013

Character:
Mrs. de Winter

American actress born Joan de Beauvoir de Havilland (in Japan, to British parents) who was best known for her starring roles in cinema during the Classical Hollywood era. Fontaine appeared in more than 45 feature films in a career that spanned five decades. She was nominated three times for an Academy Award, winning once for her role in Alfred Hitchcock's Suspicion (1941) - her other nominated roles were in the films Rebecca and The Constant Nymph (1943).

George Sanders
Born: July 3, 1906
Died: April 25, 1972

Character:
Jack Favell

Film and television actor, singer-songwriter, music composer, and author. His career as an actor spanned over forty years. His upper-class English accent and bass voice often led him to be cast as sophisticated but villainous characters. He is perhaps best known for his roles in Rebecca, Foreign Correspondent (1940), All About Eve (1950), for which he won an Academy Award, and as Simon Templar, 'The Saint', in five films made in the 1930s and 1940s.

TRIVIA

Goofs At the inquest when Ben begins to testify the clock reads 11:48, but a few minutes later when Mr. de Winter is recalled it reads 1:53. Shortly after, when Mrs de Winter faints, the clock reads 11:48 once again.

The large map on the courtroom wall depicts the Americas and as such it is implausible that it would be displayed on the wall of an English courtroom.

Interesting Facts Rebecca was the first movie that Sir Alfred Hitchcock made in Hollywood and was the only one that won a Best Picture Academy Award. His other Oscar nominated works were Lifeboat (1944), Spellbound (1945), Rear Window (1954) and Psycho (1960).

CONTINUED

Interesting Facts Over twenty actresses were screen-tested for the role of Mrs. de Winter, which eventually went to newcomer Joan Fontaine.

Because Sir Laurence Olivier wanted his then-girlfriend Vivien Leigh to play the lead role, he treated Joan Fontaine horribly. This shook Fontaine up quite a bit, so Sir Alfred Hitchcock decided to capitalize on this by telling her everyone on the set hated her, thus making her shy and uneasy, just what he wanted from her performance.

Filming started five days after the U.K. entered World War II. This proved to be particularly troublesome to Sir Alfred Hitchcock and the movie's largely British cast.

Due to the success of this movie in Spain the specific jackets worn by Joan Fontaine during filming began to be known as 'rebecas'. The word is still used nowadays to refer to this item of clothing.

Quote **Maxim de Winter:** I can't forget what it's done to you. I've been thinking of nothing else since it happened. It's gone forever, that funny young, lost look I loved won't ever come back. I killed that when I told you about Rebecca. It's gone. In a few hours, you've grown so much older.

THE PHILADELPHIA STORY

Directed by: George Cukor - Runtime: 1 hour 52 minutes

When a rich woman's ex-husband and a tabloid-type reporter turn up just before her planned remarriage, she begins to learn the truth about herself.

STARRING

Cary Grant
Born: January 18, 1904
Died: November 29, 1986

Character:
C. K. Dexter Haven

British-American actor (born Archibald Alec Leach) known as one of classic Hollywood's definitive leading men. He began a career in Hollywood in the early 1930s and became known for his transatlantic accent, light-hearted approach to acting, comic timing and debonair demeanour. He was twice nominated for the Academy Award for Best Actor for his roles in Penny Serenade (1941) and None But The Lonely Heart (1944).

Katharine Hepburn
Born: May 12, 1907
Died: June 29, 2003

Character:
Tracy Lord

American actress known for her fierce independence and spirited personality. Hepburn was a leading lady in Hollywood for more than 60 years and appeared in a range of genres from screwball comedy to literary drama, and she received a record of four Academy Awards for Best Actress. In 1999, Hepburn was named by the American Film Institute as the greatest female star of Classic Hollywood Cinema.

James Stewart
Born: May 20, 1908
Died: July 2, 1997

Character:
Macaulay Connor

Actor and military officer who is among the most honored and popular stars in film history. With a career spanning 62 years, Stewart was nominated for five Academy Awards, winning one for The Philadelphia Story and receiving another, a Lifetime Achievement award, in 1985. In 1999, Stewart was named the third-greatest male screen legend of the Golden Age of Hollywood by the American Film Institute, behind Humphrey Bogart and Cary Grant.

TRIVIA

Goofs	When CK Dexter-Haven is whistling after coming to the mansion, Mrs. Lord calls Tracy 'Kathy' instead of Tracy.
	As Connor and Tracy exit the library the boom mic is reflected on the windshield of Tracy's car.
Interesting Facts	James Stewart never felt he deserved the Oscar for his performance in this film, especially since he had initially felt miscast. He always maintained that Henry Fonda should have won instead for The Grapes Of Wrath (1940), and that the award was probably 'deferred payment for his work on Mr. Smith Goes To Washington (1939)'.

CONTINUED

Interesting Facts | Cary Grant demanded top billing and $100,000 salary, a huge amount at the time. As it turned out, however, he donated his entire earnings to the British War Relief Fund.

Katharine Hepburn starred in the Broadway production of the play on which this film was based and owned the film rights to the material; they were purchased for her by billionaire Howard Hughes, then given to her as a gift.

James Stewart wasn't at all comfortable with some of the dialog, especially in the swimming pool scene, which also required him to act in a dressing gown. He said at the time that if he'd played the scene in just a swimming costume it would have been the end of his career.

Quotes | **C. K. Dexter Haven:** Sometimes, for your own sake, Red, I think you should've stuck to me longer.
Tracy Lord: I thought it was for life, but the nice judge gave me a full pardon.
C. K. Dexter Haven: Aaah, that's the old redhead. No bitterness, no recrimination, just a good swift left to the jaw.

Macaulay Connor: Oh Tracy darling...
Tracy Lord: Mike...
Macaulay Connor: What can I say to you? Tell me darling.
Tracy Lord: Not anything - don't say anything. And especially not 'darling'.

Tracy Lord: The time to make up your mind about people is never.

THE GRAPES OF WRATH

Directed by: John Ford - Runtime: 2 hours 9 minutes

After their drought-ridden farm is seized by the bank the Joad family, led by just-paroled son Tom, loads up a truck and heads West. On the road, beset by hardships, the Joads meet dozens of other families making the same trek and holding onto the same dream. Once in California, however, the Joads soon realize that the promised land isn't quite what they hoped.

STARRING

Henry Fonda
Born: May 16, 1905
Died: August 12, 1982

Character:
Tom Joad

Film and stage actor, Fonda made his Hollywood debut in 1935 and his career gained momentum after his Academy Award-nominated performance as Tom Joad in The Grapes Of Wrath. Throughout six decades in Hollywood he cultivated a strong appealing screen image and won an Academy Award for Best Actor for his final film role in the movie On Golden Pond (1981). In 1999, he was named the sixth-Greatest Male Star of All Time by the American Film Institute.

Jane Darwell
Born: October 15, 1879
Died: August 13, 1967

Characters:
Ma Joad

Actress of stage, film and television who appeared in more than one hundred major motion pictures spanning half a century. She is perhaps best-remembered for her poignant portrayal of the matriarch and leader of the Joad family in John Steinbeck's The Grapes Of Wrath, for which she received the Academy Award for Best Supporting Actress. In 1960 Darwell received a star on the Hollywood Walk of Fame for her contributions to the motion-picture industry.

John Carradine
Born: February 5, 1906
Died: November 27, 1988

Character:
Jim Casy

Actor, best known for his roles in horror films, Westerns and Shakespearean theatre. A member of Cecil B. DeMille's stock company and later John Ford's company, he was one of the most prolific character actors in Hollywood history and starred in over 230 films throughout his career. For his contributions to the film industry Carradine was inducted into the Hollywood Walk of Fame in 1960, and the Western Performers Hall of Fame in 2003.

TRIVIA

Goofs	One of the cars (license plate 263 with the silver bed springs sticking out of the back) evacuating the Department of Agriculture camp site leaves the camp twice, once before the Joads pack up and once after.
	When the Joads set out from the gas station to cross the desert you see them pull away from the station twice.
Interesting Facts	Writer John Steinbeck loved the movie and said that Henry Fonda as Tom Joad made him believe his own words.

CONTINUED

Interesting Facts

Prior to filming producer Darryl F. Zanuck sent undercover investigators out to the migrant camps to see if John Steinbeck had been exaggerating about the squalor and unfair treatment meted out there. He was horrified to discover that, if anything, Steinbeck had actually downplayed what went on in the camps.

Director John Ford banned all makeup and perfume from the set on the grounds that it was not in keeping with the tone of the picture.

Henry Fonda kept the hat he wore in the movie for the rest of his life, until before he passed away in 1982 when he gave it to his old friend Jane Withers. Apparently, he and Withers, when she was an 8-year-old girl and he a young man, did a play together before Fonda made it the movies. Fonda was so nervous to go onstage that little Jane took his hand, said a little prayer to ease his nerves, and the two of them became good friends for life.

Although John Carradine hated John Ford's bullying style of direction he nevertheless made eleven films with him over a period of 28 years. Ford was particularly keen on Carradine's unusual look.

Quote

[last lines]
Ma Joad: Rich fellas come up an' they die, an' their kids ain't no good an' they die out. But we keep a'comin'. We're the people that live. They can't wipe us out; they can't lick us. We'll go on forever, Pa, 'cause we're the people.

THE GREAT DICTATOR

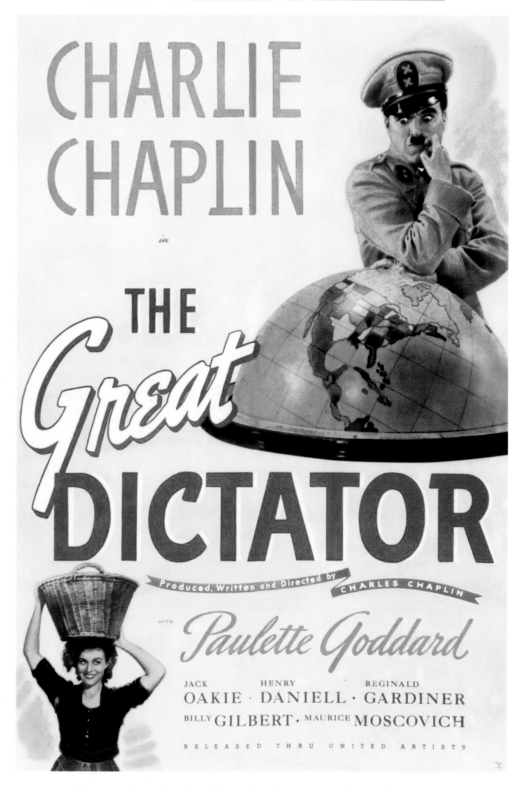

Directed by: Charles Chaplin - Runtime: 2 hours 5 minutes

Dictator Adenoid Hynkel tries to expand his empire while a poor Jewish barber tries to avoid persecution from Hynkel's regime.

STARRING

Charlie Chaplin
Born: April 16, 1889
Died: December 25, 1977

Character:
Hynkel - Dictator of
Tomania / A Jewish Barber

Sir Charles Spencer 'Charlie' Chaplin was an English comic actor, filmmaker and composer who rose to fame in the silent era. Chaplin became a worldwide icon through his screen persona 'the Tramp' and is considered one of the most important figures in the history of the film industry. His career spanned more than 75 years from his childhood in Victorian England until a year before his death in 1977.

Paulette Goddard
Born: June 3, 1910
Died: April 23, 1990

Character:
Hannah

Goddard was a child fashion model and performer in several Broadway productions as a Ziegfeld Girl. She became a major star for Paramount Studios in the 1940s and her most notable films were as Charles Chaplin's leading lady in Modern Times (her first major role) and his subsequent film The Great Dictator. She was nominated for an Academy Award for Best Supporting Actress for her performance in So Proudly We Hail! (1943).

Jack Oakie
Born: November 12, 1903
Died: January 23, 1978

Character:
Napaloni - Dictator of
Bacteria

Actor, starring mostly in films but also on stage, radio and television. Oakie worked in various musicals and comedies on Broadway from 1923 to 1927, before leaving to go to Hollywood to work in movies. He signed with Paramount Pictures in 1927 and made his first talking film, The Dummy, in 1929. His portrayal of Napaloni in The Great Dictator earned him a nomination for the Academy Award for Best Supporting Actor.

TRIVIA

Goofs	When the Barber and Schultz are flying upside down, the wire waving Schultz's scarf can be seen.
	When the barber slides into the basement window while evading the stormtrooper, his hat falls off onto the street. In the next shot he is wearing his hat again.
Interesting Facts	According to documentaries on the making of the film, Charles Chaplin began to feel more uncomfortable lampooning Adolf Hitler the more he heard of Hitler's actions in Europe. Ultimately, the invasion of France inspired Chaplin to change the ending of his film to include his famous speech.

CONTINUED

Interesting Facts

Adolf Hitler banned the film in Germany and in all countries occupied by the Nazis. Curiosity got the best of him though and he had a print brought in through Portugal. History records that he screened it twice, in private, but history did not record his reaction to the film. Chaplin said, "I'd give anything to know what he thought of it." For political reasons in Germany the ban stayed in place after the end of WWII and until 1958.

The film was released eleven years after the end of the silent era and was Chaplin's first all-talking, all-sound film. It was financed entirely by Chaplin and was his biggest box-office hit.

The German spoken by the dictator is complete nonsense and was improvised. The language in which the shop signs, posters, etc in the Jewish quarter are written is Esperanto, a language created in 1887 by Dr L.L. Zamenhof, a Polish Jew.

Quotes

Schultz: Strange, and I always thought of you as an Aryan.
A Jewish Barber: I'm a vegetarian

Madame Napaloni: *[arriving at the Tomainia train station]* Papa, why can't-a we get out here?
Napaloni - Dictator of Bacteria: There is-a no carpet.
Madame Napaloni: Who cares about a carpet?
Napaloni - Dictator of Bacteria: Il Digaditchi, me, a-Napaloni, I never get out without a carpet!

Adenoid Hynkel: Ah, de Aryan. Und de Aryan maiden. Ah, de Aryan maiden! Ah, the delicatessen bitte schön.

PINOCCHIO

Directors: Ben Sharpsteen / Hamilton Luske - Runtime: 1 hour 28 minutes

A living puppet, with the help of a cricket as his conscience, must prove himself worthy to become a real boy.

TRIVIA

Goofs

Pinocchio and Lampwick are seen hanging out together playing eight ball pool, but eight ball pool didn't exist until around 1908 and this film is presumably set in the 19th century.

When Pinocchio plays with the candle he burns his left hand but Gepetto puts Pinocchio's right hand into the water.

Interesting Facts

Walt Disney insisted that the identities of all the actors and singers providing the voices for his characters were kept secret. He believed that if audiences knew who was providing the voice that the magic would be ruined.

Figaro the cat was Walt Disney's favourite character. Disney pushed for the kitten to appear in the film as much as possible.

Originally budgeted at $500,000, the development of the film caused it to go way over budget and ultimately cost $2.5 million, one of the most expensive films ever produced at the time.

The theme song from Pinocchio, "When You Wish Upon A Star", was ranked No.7 in the 2004 American Film Institute's List of the Top Movie Songs of All Time, the highest-ranking song on the list among Disney animated films.

Pinocchio was the first animated film to win an Academy Award in a competitive category; Snow White And The Seven Dwarfs (1937) had won a Special Academy Award two years earlier.

Quotes

The Blue Fairy: A lie keeps growing and growing until it's as plain as the nose on your face.

Jiminy Cricket: You buttered your bread. Now sleep in it!

The Blue Fairy: Prove yourself brave, truthful, and unselfish, and someday, you will be a real boy.

SPORTING WINNERS

TOM HARMON - COLLEGE FOOTBALL

AP Associated Press - MALE ATHLETE OF THE YEAR

Thomas Dudley Harmon
Born: September 28, 1919 in Rensselaer, Indiana
Died: March 15, 1990 in Los Angeles, California
NFL Draft: 1941 / Round: 1 / Pick: 1
Career History: Los Angeles Rams (1946-1947)

Tom Harmon, sometimes known by the nickname 'Old 98', was a football player, military pilot, actor, and sports broadcaster.

Harmon grew up in Gary, Indiana, and played college football at the halfback position for the University of Michigan from 1938 to 1940. He led the nation in scoring and was a consensus All-American in both 1939 and 1940. In 1940 he also won the Heisman Trophy, the Maxwell Award, and the Associated Press Athlete of the Year award. Harmon was inducted into the College Football Hall of Fame in 1954.

Career Highlights / Awards:

1938 - 1940	First-Team All-Big Ten
1940	Big Ten MVP
1940	Heisman Trophy
1940	Maxwell Award
1939 - 1940	Consensus All-American
1940	Associated Press Male Athlete Of The Year
1962	Michigan Sports Hall of Fame

ALICE MARBLE - TENNIS

AP Associated Press - FEMALE ATHLETE OF THE YEAR

Alice Marble
Born: September 28, 1913 in Beckwourth, California
Died: December 13, 1990 in Palm Springs, California
Tennis World No.1: 1939

Alice Marble was a World No.1 American tennis player who won 18 Grand Slam championships from 1936 through 1940; five in singles, six in women's doubles and seven in mixed doubles. She was included in the year-end top ten rankings issued by the United States Lawn Tennis Association in 1932-1933 and 1936-1940, and was the top-ranked U.S. player from 1936 to 1940. Marble was also the Associated Press Female Athlete of the Year on two occasions (1939 and 1940).

Tennis Titles:

Grand Slam Singles	Wimbledon	1939
	U.S. Open	1936 / 1938 / 1939 / 1940
Grand Slam Doubles	Wimbledon	1938 / 1939
	U.S. Open	1937 / 1938 / 1939 / 1940
Grand Slam Mixed Doubles	Wimbledon	1937 / 1938 / 1939
	U.S. Open	1936 / 1938 / 1939 / 1940
Team Competitions	Wightman Cup	1933 / 1937 / 1938 / 1939

In 1940 after capping off a stellar amateur career Marble turned professional and earned more than $100,000 travelling around playing exhibition tournaments. In 1964 she was inducted into the International Tennis Hall of Fame and afterwards settled in Palm Desert, California, where she taught tennis until her death aged 77.

GOLF

THE MASTERS - JIMMY DEMARET

The Masters Tournament is the first of the majors to be played each year and unlike the other major championships it is played at the same location - Augusta National Golf Club, Georgia. Jimmy Demaret won the first of his three Masters titles (also 1947 and 1950), four strokes ahead of runner-up Lloyd Mangrum, to take home the $1,500 winner's share of the $5,000 prize fund.

PGA CHAMPIONSHIP - BYRON NELSON

The 1940 and 23rd PGA Championship was played at Hershey Country Club in Hershey, Pennsylvania. Then a match play championship Byron Nelson won his first PGA Championship defeating Sam Snead 1 up in the 36-hole final. It was the third of Nelson's five major titles and his first PGA Championship win (he would win it again in 1945). The total prize fund for the competition was $11,050 of which Nelson took home $1,100.

U.S. OPEN - LAWSON LITTLE

The U.S. Open Championship (established in 1895) was held June 6-9 at Canterbury Golf Club in Beachwood, Ohio, a suburb east of Cleveland. Lawson Little defeated Gene Sarazen in an 18-hole playoff to win his only professional major and $1,000 in prize money. The top eight finishers in the tournament were all past or future major champions and members of the World Golf Hall of Fame.

Lawson Little

Jimmy Demaret

Byron Nelson

WORLD SERIES - CINCINNATI REDS

Cincinnati Reds   4 - 3   Detroit Tigers

Total attendance: 281,927 - Average attendance: 40,275
Winning player's share: $5,804 - Losing player's share: $3,532

The 1940 World Series matched the Cincinnati Reds against the Detroit Tigers, the Reds winning a closely contested seven-game series for their second championship 21 years after their scandal-tainted victory in 1919. This would be the Reds' last World Series championship win for 35 years despite appearances in 1961, 1970, and 1972.

Series Summary:

Game	Date	Score			Location	Time	Att.
1	Oct 2	**Detroit Tigers**	7-2	Cincinnati Reds	Crosley Field	2:09	31,793
2	Oct 3	Detroit Tigers	3-5	**Cincinnati Reds**	Crosley Field	1:54	30,640
3	Oct 4	Cincinnati Reds	4-7	**Detroit Tigers**	Briggs Stadium	2:08	52,877
4	Oct 5	**Cincinnati Reds**	5-2	Detroit Tigers	Briggs Stadium	2:06	54,093
5	Oct 6	Cincinnati Reds	0-8	**Detroit Tigers**	Briggs Stadium	2:26	55,189
6	Oct 7	Detroit Tigers	0-4	**Cincinnati Reds**	Crosley Field	2:01	30,481
7	Oct 8	Detroit Tigers	1-2	**Cincinnati Reds**	Crosley Field	1:47	26,854

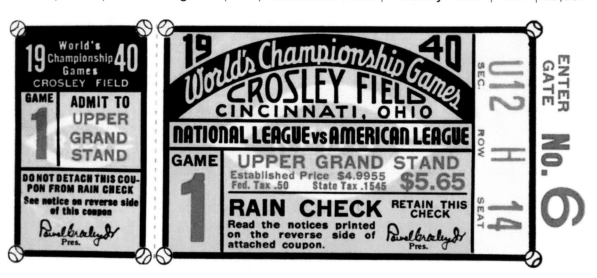

Horse Racing

Bimelech at the 1940 Kentucky Derby with Jockey Fred Smith.

Bimelech (1937-1966) was an American Hall of Fame Thoroughbred racehorse who won two Triple Crown races and was both the American Champion 2-Year-Old Colt in 1939, and American Champion 3-Year-Old Male Horse in 1940. Bimelech was undefeated as a two-year-old and was the overwhelming choice for the 1940 Kentucky Derby at odds of 3 to 1. In the Derby he drifted out from the rail and ran wide the entire race. The longer distance left him exhausted and Gallahadion passed him in the final furlong - jockey Fred Smith took the blame for the loss. Bimelch proceeded to win both the Preakness and Belmont stakes, and retired with career earnings of $248,745.

Kentucky Derby - Gallahadion

The Kentucky Derby is held annually at Churchill Downs in Louisville, Kentucky on the first Saturday in May. The race is a Grade 1 stakes race for three-year-olds and is one and a quarter mile in length.

Preakness Stakes - Bimelech

The Preakness Stakes is held on the third Saturday in May each year at Pimlico Race Course in Baltimore, Maryland. It is a Grade 1 race run over a distance of 9.5 furlongs (1 3/16 miles) on dirt.

Belmont Stakes - Bimelech

The Belmont Stakes is Grade 1 race held every June at Belmont Park in Elmont, New York. It is 1.5 miles in length and open to three-year-old thoroughbreds. It takes place on a Saturday between June 5 and June 11.

Football - NFL Championship

Championship Game

Chicago Bears

73 - 0

Washington Redskins

Played: December 8, 1940 at Griffith Stadium, Washington, D.C. - Attendance: 36,034

The 1940 NFL season was the 21st regular season of the National Football League. The season ended when the Chicago Bears scored eleven touchdowns to defeat the Washington Redskins 73-0 in the Championship Game. This game still stands as the most one-sided victory in NFL history.

Division Results:

Eastern Division

Team	P	W	L	T	PCT	PF	PA
Washington Redskins	**11**	**9**	**2**	**0**	**.818**	**245**	**142**
Brooklyn Dodgers	11	8	3	0	.727	186	120
New York Giants	11	6	4	1	.600	131	133
Pittsburgh Steelers	11	2	7	2	.222	60	178
Philadelphia Eagles	11	1	10	0	.091	111	211

Western Division

Team	P	W	L	T	PCT	PF	PA
Chicago Bears	**11**	**8**	**3**	**0**	**.727**	**238**	**152**
Green Bay Packers	11	6	4	1	.600	238	155
Detroit Lions	11	5	5	1	.500	138	153
Cleveland Rams	11	4	6	1	.400	171	191
Chicago Cardinals	11	2	7	2	.222	139	222

Note: The NFL did not officially count tie games in the standings until 1972.
Joe F. Carr Trophy (Most Valuable Player) - Ace Parker - Brooklyn

League Leaders

Statistic	Name	Team	Yards
Passing	Sammy Baugh	Washington	1367
Rushing	Whizzer White	Detroit	514
Receiving	Don Looney	Philadelphia	707

Hockey: 1939-1940 NHL Season

The 1939-1940 NHL season was the 23rd season of the National Hockey League and included seven teams each playing 48 games. The Boston Bruins were the best in the regular season but the Stanley Cup winners were the New York Rangers who took their third championship trophy in 14 seasons of existence. It would be another 54 years before they would win again.

Final Standings:

	Team	GP	W	L	T	GF	GA	PIM	Pts
1	**Boston Bruins**	**48**	**31**	**12**	**5**	**170**	**98**	**330**	**67**
2	New York Rangers	48	27	11	10	136	77	520	64
3	Toronto Maple Leafs	48	25	17	6	134	110	485	56
4	Chicago Black Hawks	48	23	19	6	112	120	351	52
5	Detroit Red Wings	48	16	26	6	90	126	250	38
6	New York Americans	48	15	29	4	106	140	236	34
7	Montreal Canadiens	48	10	33	5	90	167	338	25

Scoring Leaders:

	Player	Team	GP	Goals	Assists	Pts
1	**Milt Schmidt**	**Boston Bruins**	**48**	**22**	**30**	**52**
2	Woody Dumart	Boston Bruins	48	22	21	43
3	Bobby Bauer	Boston Bruins	48	17	26	43

Hart Trophy (Most Valuable Player): Ebbie Goodfellow - Detroit Red Wings
Vezina Trophy (Fewest Goals Allowed): Dave Kerr - New York Rangers

Stanley Cup

New York Rangers

4 - 2

Toronto Maple Leafs

Series Summary:

Game:	①	②	③	④	⑤	⑥
New York Rangers	**2**	**6**	**1**	**0**	**2**	**3**
Toronto Maple Leafs	1	2	2	3	1	2
Date:	Apr 2	Apr 3	Apr 6	Apr 9	Apr 11	Apr 13

INDIANAPOLIS 500 - WILBUR SHAW

Wilbur Shaw and his 1940 Indy 500 winning Maserati 8CTF.

The 28th International 500-Mile Sweepstakes Race was held at the Indianapolis Motor Speedway on May 30, 1940. The race was won by the No.1 car of Wilbur Shaw with an average speed of 114.277mph (slowed by rain which caused the last 50 laps to be run under caution). This was Shaw's third of three Indy 500 wins and he completed it in the same Maserati 8CTF he had driven to victory in 1939; his other win was in 1937. Shaw took home $31,875 in prize winnings (equivalent to $573,094 in 2019), plus additional prizes that included a car and a refrigerator.

BOSTON MARATHON

The Boston Marathon is the oldest annual marathon in the world and dates back to 1897. It is always held on Patriots' Day, the third Monday of April, and was inspired by the success of the first marathon competition in the 1896 Summer Olympics.

The 1940 Boston Marathon was won by Gérard Côté, the first of his 4 victories in the race (he would win it again in 1943, 1944 and 1948). Côté set a new course record with his time of 2h 28m 28s and was awarded the Lou Marsh Trophy as Canada's top athlete of the year.

1. **Gérard Côté (CAN)**   **2:28:28**
2. John A. Kelley (USA)   2:32:00
3. Don Heinicke (USA)   2:32:21

TENNIS - U.S. NATIONAL CHAMPIONSHIPS

Ladies Singles Champion - Alice Marble / Men's Singles Champion - Donald McNeill.

The 1940 U.S. National Championships (now known as the U.S. Open) took place on the outdoor grass courts at the West Side Tennis Club, Forest Hills in New York. The tournament ran from September 2 through September 9 and was the 60th staging of the Championships. *N.B. In 1940 both Wimbledon and the French Grand Slams were cancelled due to World War II.*

Men's Singles Final

Country	Player	Set 1	Set 2	Set 3	Set 4	Set 5
United States	Donald McNeill	4	6	6	6	7
United States	Bobby Riggs	6	8	3	3	5

Women's Singles Final

Country	Player	Set 1	Set 2
United States	Alice Marble	6	6
United States	Helen Jacobs	2	3

Men's Doubles Final

Country	Players	Set 1	Set 2	Set 3
United States	Jack Kramer / Ted Schroeder	6	8	9
United States	Gardnar Mulloy / Henry Prussoff	4	6	7

Women's Doubles Final

Country	Players	Set 1	Set 2
United States	Sarah Palfrey Cooke / Alice Marble	6	6
United States	Dorothy Bundy / Marjorie Gladman Van Ryn	4	4

Mixed Doubles Final

Country	Players	Set 1	Set 2
United States	Alice Marble / Bobby Riggs	9	6
United States	Dorothy Bundy / Jack Kramer	7	1

THE COST OF LIVING

COMPARISON CHART

	1940	1940 + Inflation	2019	% Change
House	$8,850	$159,118	$309,700	+94.6%
Annual Income	$1,050	$18,878	$61,372	+225.1%
Car	$1,350	$24,272	$34,000	+40.1%
Gallon of Gasoline	15¢	$2.70	$2.70	0%
Gallon of Milk	18¢	$3.24	$3.28	+1.2%
DC Comic Book	10¢	$1.80	$3.99	+121.7%

GROCERIES

Parker House Rolls (doz.)	15¢
Golden State Butter (per lb)	36¢
Sunny Valley Large Grade A Eggs (doz.)	34¢
White House Evaporated Milk (4 tall cans)	23¢
C&H Cane Sugar (10lb cloth bag)	51¢
Ace-Hi Flour (24½lb sack)	76¢
Longhorn Cheese (per lb)	25¢
Kraft Cheese (2lb loaf)	48¢
Wheat Puffs (pkg.)	4¢
Sunny-Field Corn Flakes (2x 8oz pkg.)	11¢
Skippy Peanut Butter (1lb jar)	19¢
Bananas (5lbs)	19¢
California Oranges (3 doz.)	25¢
Oak Glen Apples (7lb)	25¢
Thompson Seedless Grapes (3lbs)	10¢
Santa Rosa Plums (4lbs)	10¢
Watermelon (per lb)	1¢
Del Monte Tomatoes (2x No.2½ cans)	25¢
Lettuce (x3)	5¢
White Rose Potatoes (100lb sack)	69¢
Cabbage (6lbs)	5¢
Sweet Italian Onions (3lb)	5¢
Sweet Corn (x12)	10¢
Green Giant Peas (17oz tin)	12¢
Beef Roast (per lb)	15¢
Lamb Leg (per lb)	24¢
Minced Sliced Ham (per lb)	15¢
Pure Pork Roast (per lb)	15¢
Swift Premium Bacon (per lb)	23¢
Fresh Dressed Rabbits (per lb)	29¢
Fresh Killed Turkeys (per lb)	17¢
Stewing Hens (per lb)	19¢
Libby's Corned Beef (12oz tin)	17½¢
Perfect Strike Alaska Salmon (No.1 can)	13¢
Rio Del Mar Sardines (2 tins)	15¢
Lipton's Tea (per lb)	79¢
Folger's Coffee (1lb vacuum tin)	24¢
Red Circle Coffee (1lb bag)	18¢
Ovaltine (small tin)	34¢
Pepsi-Cola (6 bottle carton)	25¢
Coca-Cola (bottle)	5¢
Campbell's Tomato Juice (3x 20oz can)	23¢
Fitch Shampoo	59¢
Floss-Tex Toilet Tissue (3 rolls)	11¢
Kleenex Tissues (150 count)	10¢
Colgate Ribbon Dental Cream (x2)	29¢
White King Granulated Soap (family pkg.)	23¢
Vick's Vapo-Rub	27¢

"Relax...take it easy"

Coca-Cola has the charm of purity. It is prepared with the finished art that comes from a lifetime of practice. Its delicious taste never loses the freshness of appeal that first delighted you...always bringing you a cool, clean sense of complete refreshment. Thirst asks nothing more.

Drink

Coca-Cola
TRADE MARK REG U S PAT OFF

Delicious and Refreshing

5¢

An easy way to take things easy is to take an ice-cold bottle of Coca-Cola...raise it to your lips... and enjoy *the pause that refreshes*. It's a refreshing short-cut to relaxation. And it's easy to do . . . anywhere. Enjoy an ice-cold Coca-Cola, now.

THE PAUSE THAT REFRESHES

63

CLOTHES

Women's Clothing

Harris Tweed Coat	$16.95
Markell's 'Shorty' Coat	$5.95
Straw Hat	$1
Kayser Gloves	10¢
'Roncho' Cloth Slack Suit	$3.95
Markell's Success Frock	$3.95
French Batiste Blouse	$3.98
Tailored Taffeta Slip	59¢
Warner's Alphabet Brassieres	$1
Lady Myna Silk Hosiery	79¢
Harris Silk Briefs	75¢
Rayon Panties	15¢
Nurses Oxford Shoes	$1.99

Men's Clothing

Melton Jacket	$1.98
Harris All Wool Tropical Suit	$11
McGregor Sport Suit	$16.50
McGregor Slipover Sweater	$3.50
Harris Long Sleeve Sports Shirt	$1.19
Plaid Work Shirt	89¢
Crew Neck Tee Shirt	39¢
Harris Summer Slacks	$3.98
Harris Broadcloth Pyjamas	$1.69
Stoner's Slippers	87¢
Work Sox (pair)	5¢

TOYS

Sears Elgin Bike	$34.95
Speedy Velocipede	$2.98
American Flyer Train	$6.50
48in Ride 'Em Freight Train	$1.89
Tractor - Extra Large Rear Wheels	$11.95
6-Wheel Scooter Wagon	$8.95
Speed King All Steel Wagon	$3.95
Kids Steel Rocker	$1.25
Miss Sunshine Doll	$1.98
Gay And Colorful Refugee Dutch Doll	49¢
28in Stick Horse	39¢
Electric Phonograph In Carrying Case	$3.98
Toy Model Grand Piano	$1.09
Rollicking Rollover Pluto	47¢
7-piece Cleaning Set	$1
Dart Board Target And Darts	$1.19
Playing Cards	29¢

The "Petty Girl" suit of 1940

BY JANTZEN

A great artist turns to swim suit design! With the same master strokes in simplicity of line that have made him so famous with brush and canvas. Here's George Petty's conception of the Suit of Youth, classic in design with slenderizing princess lines.

Tailored by Jantzen in a perfectly amazing new fabric, *Sea Ripple*. A swim suit that actually stretches all ways! A swim suit with real foundation garment control! It fits as you have never known a swim suit could fit. See it—feel it—try it on. Lastex* yarn has been knitted-in for perfect figure-molding. There's a new experience in beauty of line and perfection of fit awaiting you. In the new fashionable colors—$6.95 in U.S.A. For illustrated style folder, men's or women's, address Dept. 321.

A reproduction of this Petty Painting without advertising copy will be sent on receipt of 10c in stamps or coin.

JANTZEN KNITTING MILLS, PORTLAND, OREGON; VANCOUVER, CANADA

*Reg. U.S. Pat. Off.

Jantzen

SWIM SUITS AND SUN CLOTHES

- IF YOU LIKE SMOOTH CURVES YOU'LL LOVE THIS SUIT -
George PETTY

© JANTZEN KNITTING MILLS, 1940

OTHER ITEMS

Cadillac LaSalle	$1,240
Nash Ambassador 600 Four Door Sedan	$939
Chevrolet Station Wagon	$903
Dodge Luxury Liner 2 Door Sedan	$860
Super Body Motor Oil (2 gallon can)	$1.09
Cornell Cavalcade Tires (size 6.00-16)	$6.25
Montgomery Ward Refrigerator (6.4 cubic foot)	$133
Philco Transitone Radio	$14.95
6-Tube Remington Auto Radio	$19.95
Underwoods 'Like New' Typewriter	$44.95
Manning And Bowman Sandwich Toaster	$7.95
53-Piece Dinner Set	$9.85
Sheriff's Pride Of Dundee Scotch (fifth)	$2.59
Hiram Walker's Deluxe Straight Bourbon Whiskey (pint)	$1.22
Piper's Dry Gin (fifth)	$1.12
Brownie Pilsner Beer (24x 11oz bottle)	$1.15

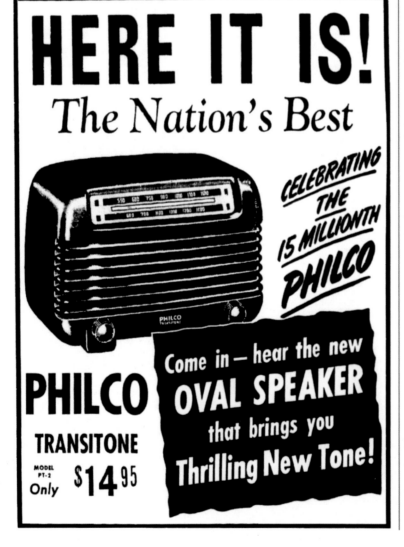

"It's a NATURAL!"

Eye It!

You have only to *eye* this new Chevrolet with its smoothly modeled Body by Fisher and smartly streamlined "Royal Clipper" Styling to know that it's the most *beautiful* car of the year . . . that it's the *longest* of all lowest-priced cars . . . and that it's also the most *luxurious* car in the low-price field, with item after item of de luxe equipment at no extra cost!

181 INCHES FROM FRONT OF GRILLE TO REAR OF BODY

The Special De Luxe Town Sedan, $761*

AMONG LOWEST-PRICED CARS

"THE LONGEST OF THE LOT"

ONLY CAR WITH VACUUM-POWER SHIFT

Try It!

You have only to *try* the new Chevrolet to know that it *out-accelerates, out-climbs* and *out-performs* all other low-priced cars . . . that it's the *easiest* car to drive, because it alone has the Vacuum-Power Shift, which supplies 80% of the gearshifting effort—*automatically* . . . and that it's also the *easiest-riding* car in its price range—the *only* car with "The Ride Royal"★— the smoothest, safest, steadiest ride known!

The Special De Luxe Business Coupe, $720*

OUT-ACCELERATES and OUT-CLIMBS THE FIELD

Buy It!

You have only to *buy* a new Chevrolet to know that it gives the greatest all-round satisfaction at the greatest all-round saving . . . and that this is why it's *out-selling* all other makes of cars for the ninth time in the last ten years!

★On Special De Luxe and Master De Luxe Series.

$659
MASTER 85 BUSINESS COUPE
Other models slightly higher

*All models priced at Flint, Michigan. Transportation based on rail rates, state and local taxes (if any), optional equipment and accessories—extra. Prices subject to change without notice.

"CHEVROLET'S FIRST AGAIN!"

CHEVROLET MOTOR DIVISION, *General Motors Sales Corporation,* DETROIT, MICHIGAN

67

U.S. COINS

Official Circulated U.S. Coins		Years Produced
Half-Cent	½¢	1792 - 1857
Cent (Penny)	1¢	1793 - Present
2-Cent	2¢	1864 - 1873
3-Cent	3¢	1851 - 1889
Half-Dime	5¢	1792 - 1873
Five Cent Nickel	5¢	1866 - Present
Dime	10¢	1792 - Present
20-Cent	20¢	1875 - 1878
Quarter	25¢	1796 - Present
Half Dollar	50¢	1794 - Present
Dollar Coin	$1	1794 - Present
Quarter Eagle	$2.50	1792 - 1929
Three-Dollar Piece	$3	1854 - 1889
Four-Dollar Piece	$4	1879 - 1880
Half Eagle	$5	1795 – 1929
Commemorative Half Eagle	$5	1980 - Present
Silver Eagle	$1	1986 - Present
Gold Eagle	$5	1986 - Present
Platinum Eagle	$10 - $100	1997 - Present
Double Eagle (Gold)	$20	1849 - 1933
Half Union	$50	1915

THE OUTSTANDING TRUCK FOR THE MONEY

FORD V·8 FOR 1940

FORD FEATURES FOR 1940

New styling · Increased engine accessibility · Increased chassis accessibility · Choice of power—95, 85, 60 hp · 42 body and chassis types · New Sealed-Beam Headlamps · Bigger batteries, larger generators with automatic voltage regulation · Big hydraulic brakes · Full-floating rear axle with straddle-mounted pinion and ring gear thrust plate · Two-speed axle (optional at extra cost) · Ford Engine and Parts Exchange Plan.

The big new 1940 Ford Truck line gives you value in construction, performance and economy that means "the outstanding truck for the money."

Three eight-cylinder engine sizes—95, 85 and 60 hp. Six wheelbases. 42 body and chassis types.

There's new styling. New engine and chassis accessibility, making it easier to check the oil, service the distributor and other engine accessories, as well as clutch, transmission and rear axle. New, softer, more comfortable seats in Regular cabs. These and many more improvements join a host of time-tested, time-proved Ford features in 1940.

See the new Ford Truck at your dealer's. Compare it with any other truck. Arrange for an "on-the-job" test and know the difference before you spend another truck dollar.

Ford Motor Company, Builders of Ford V-8 and Mercury Cars, Ford Trucks, Commercial Cars, Station Wagons, Transit Buses

Made in the USA
Columbia, SC
28 July 2020